Solo Girl

Andrea Davis Pinkney

ILLUSTRATED BY Nneka Bennett

 HOUGHTON MIFFLIN

BOSTON • MORRIS PLAINS, NJ

California • Colorado • Georgia • Illinois • New Jersey • Texas

*For my daughter Chloe, my one-of-a-kind.
And for my nieces, Gloria, Charnelle,
Victoria, and Rian—A. D. P.*

Contents

1

Blessed with the Numbers Gift

Ma Lettie called from the upstairs window. "Cass, don't you stray too far, now. You're still learning these streets." Ma Lettie's holler mixed with the noise coming from Haskins Row, one block over.

Cass and her family had just moved to the neighborhood, where Cass didn't know a soul. Well, she of course knew Ma Lettie, her foster mother, and her twin brothers, Jackson and Bud. But they didn't count. They were family—friends by relation.

"I'll stay close, Ma Lettie, I promise," Cass called back.

As she walked to the corner, Cass swung her lucky whistle. Back home, Cass had won the silver whistle in an end-of-the-school-year math bee. She had been the best math student in the whole second grade. She was smarter in math than most *third* graders, even Jackson and Bud.

Cass knew her times tables as sure as she knew her own name, and she could reel them off faster than a jazz-band drumroll.

"Three times five—fifteen!"

"Nine times four—thirty-six!"

"Seven times eight—fifty-six!"

And that wasn't all. Cass could do division in her head; she could count by twos; and she always knew how much change she was owed when she went to the store for Ma Lettie.

Ma Lettie was always saying, "The good Lord has blessed my Cass with the numbers gift." And that's what Ma Lettie asked the jeweler to put on the whistle after Cass won it—"Blessed with the numbers gift."

Cass kept her whistle on a string around her neck. She wore it proudly, as if it were a million-dollar pendant. Sometimes, Cass blew her own whistle music, little toots that helped her memorize her times tables while she walked.

"Five times five is twenty-five." *Toot-toot-toot-toot-toot-toot-toot.*

"Seven times seven is forty-nine." *Toot-toot-toot-toot-toot-toot-toot.*

"Four times eight is thirty-two." *Toot-toot-toot-toot-toot-toot.*

Cass's whistle helped her numbers gift grow.

As far as times tables went, nobody, not even Jackson or Bud, could mess with Cass. When her brothers heard her whistle toots coming down the street, they knew Cass was making math music.

"Quick—three times three!" Bud would say.

Without blinking, Cass would answer, "Three times three is nine."

"Three times three—*times three*," Jackson would say.

Cass would think really fast, and the answer would come. "Twenty-seven."

Cass didn't shy away from math problems. But when it came to playground stuff—kickball, hopscotch, and jump rope—Cass was as shy as they come. Shy because she had slow feet.

2

The Fast Feet Four

When Cass got to Haskins Row, she saw what all the noise had been about. There was some cool rope jumping going on. And one girl—boy, was she ever good. Her name was Pearl. She had long legs, fast feet, and shoelaces as pink as Ma Lettie's window flowers. She could jump rope faster than anyone on Haskins Row. She jumped double Dutch. Two ropes spinning at the same time.

When Pearl jumped, everyone gathered to watch. They shouted, "You go, Pearl! Jump! Faster, faster!" And that's what Pearl did. She jumped so fast, Cass could hardly

see her feet or legs. "I was born to jump!" Pearl shouted.

Pearl's friends, Vicky, Robin, and Tammy, had fast feet too. They called themselves the Fast Feet Four. And when they jumped, they sang the Fast Feet Four song. It went like this:

We call ourselves the Fast Feet Four.
When you see us jump, you'll ask for more.
Jump, jump, jump, till the day is done.
Jammin' with the ropes—
Got two, not one!

Since Pearl was the best jumper, the Fast Feet Four had made her their leader. Pearl taught her friends all her double-Dutch moves, and because of these slick steps, Vicky, Robin, Tammy, and Pearl were the best jumpers in town.

The Fast Feet Four gave special names to each jump. There was Red Beans' n Rice, the Skip-Hop Stop, and the High-Fly Pumpkin Pie.

"They're kickin'!" said Angela, who spun ropes for the Fast Feet Four.

"Slick as a griddle!" said Dina, another rope twirler.

"Some talented children," said Mrs. Carter, the lady who lived in the house at the end of Haskins Row.

"Too hot to handle," called out Mr. Lamont, who sold ice cream on the corner.

Cass rubbed her whistle as she watched Pearl and her friends jump. Even on a good day, Cass had trouble jumping with *one* rope. Sometimes the rope got caught on her feet. Other times it hit her ankles. And when the rope was spinning too fast, Cass didn't even try to jump in. For her, double Dutch—two ropes—was a wish.

Cass's numbers gift didn't do a thing for her slow feet. And now, with school out for the summer, Cass couldn't use her math smarts to push away her shyness. In the summer nobody cared much about three times three *times three*. There weren't any math contests to let Cass show off her smarts.

Back home, Cass had two best friends, Shana and Loreen. Cass had helped them learn their times tables by playing her

whistle. Shana and Loreen got to be really good at math, almost as good as Cass. The girls had started their own math team, the Brain Waves. Cass was their captain.

On the playground, Shana and Loreen were always bragging about Cass's numbers gift.

"Cass can speak math, teach math, and

make math into music," Loreen would say.

Shana loved to snap her fingers and tell the other kids, "Cass is brainy beyond belief."

But the times Cass spent hanging out with Shana and Loreen were long gone.

Now, day in and day out, Cass could hear the Fast Feet Four singing their song. And she could hear the shouts and claps coming from Haskins Row:

We call ourselves the Fast Feet Four.
When you see us jump, you'll ask for more.
Jump, jump, jump, till the day is done.
Jammin' with the ropes—
Got two, not one!

The singing and happy sounds rose to the sky like the birds that circled the rooftops. Cass was too shy to join in, and too scared to ask Pearl to show her how to double Dutch.

Every day, as dusk spread its purple blanket across the sky, Cass walked home alone. She missed Loreen and Shana. And she missed the days when kids were praising *her*. While Cass walked, she tried to shrug away the loneliness that was pressing at her chest.

"Cass, supper!" she heard Ma Lettie call.

"Coming, Ma!" Cass called back. Then, looking down at her sneakers, she spoke to her feet. "I sure wish you could double Dutch," she said. "Pearl and her friends are luckier than a winning lottery ticket."

3

Something Special

At supper, Cass told Jackson, Bud, and Ma Lettie about the Fast Feet Four. "They've got all the right moves," she said.

Jackson and Bud listened closely, while Ma Lettie piled each of their plates with more mashed yams.

"Remember, Cass," Ma Lettie said, "you've got fine talents of your own."

"I wish my feet could jump as smoothly as Pearl and her friends," Cass said.

The next day, Cass took Jackson and Bud to Haskins Row so they could see the Fast Feet Four for themselves.

They gathered on the corner with all the other kids to watch the Fast Feet Four let loose their high-stepping moves.

Pearl and her friends did a special jump—Red Beans 'n Rice and the High-Fly Pumpkin Pie, together. Their double-Dutch ropes did a bop. And, as always, they chanted their Fast Feet Four song:

We call ourselves the Fast Feet Four.
When you see us jump,
you'll ask for more.
Jump, jump, jump, till the day is done.
Jammin' with the ropes—
Got two, not one!

Some kids clapped. Others stomped their feet to the beat.

"See what I mean?" Cass whispered to her brothers.

Jackson shook his head. "Yeah, they're smooth," he said.

Bud nodded. "You weren't lying, Cass. Those girls have some fancy feet."

Cass and her brothers went back to Haskins Row every afternoon to check out the Fast Feet Four. Each time, Cass folded her arms tight, wishing she could jump double Dutch. She stayed hidden in the crowd, watching Pearl and the other girls. But

Jackson and Bud moved to the front of the group to get a better look.

One morning, Cass sat on the curb, tossing bits of gravel. She had been practicing with one rope. She could make it once or twice around, but whenever she tried to jump a little bit fast, she'd lose her rhythm, and trip. Cass had nearly given up on learning to double Dutch. One rope was hard enough. When Jackson and Bud saw Cass frowning, Jackson said, "Girl, get up. What's the matter with you?"

"You know what the matter is," said Cass. "I'm a jump-rope loser. A klutz."

"And I'm the king of England," said Jackson.

"And I'm the queen of France," Bud said.

"You're acting stupid," Cass said, sucking her teeth.

"You're acting stupid, times two," said Jackson.

"Listen, Cass," Bud said, "Jackson and I figured it out."

Cass sent her brothers a sideways look. "Figured *what* out?" she wanted to know.

Jackson said, "Little sis, what you need is a beat, like Pearl and her friends have over on Haskins Row."

"Yeah, " said Bud, "you need a rhythm to help you jump."

"Something special," Jackson said, "just for you."

Cass rolled her eyes. "You guys have

come up with some dumb ideas before, but this one has got to be the dumbest. How's a beat gonna help *me*?" Cass bumped the heel of her sneaker against the curb. "What I need is new feet," she said.

Bud said, "What you *need* is to trust your big brothers."

That night Cass lay in bed. She thought about the Fast Feet Four and their moves. She thought about Jackson and Bud, and what they said about a special beat that could help her. She punched her pillow. "A really stupid idea," she muttered.

4

One of a Kind

The next day, Cass went back to her curb, back to chucking gravel. Jackson and Bud came outside. Jackson was wearing a pencil behind his ear and holding a jump rope. Bud had a pad of paper tucked under his arm.

Jackson handed Cass the jump rope. "Once Bud and I are done, you're gonna need this," he said.

"Done with what?" she wanted to know.

But Jackson and Bud didn't answer. They leaned against the side of the building, next to Cass. Bud held the notepad on

Jackson's knee. He began to write. Jackson helped him. They whispered back and forth to each other. "Try this," Cass heard Jackson say. "Yeah, that'll work," Bud whispered.

Cass tried to act cool, like she didn't care what Jackson and Bud were doing. But she kept looking over at the boys, trying to see what they were writing.

Finally, Bud set the notepad in Cass's lap. "Hey, check it out. Read this," he said. When Cass looked at the page, it was a mix of scribbles and cross-outs, with some words thrown in.

Cass read out loud, starting off slowly:

I got one rope, and that's all I need.
I'm trying my best to pick up speed.
I jump alone, while my brothers twirl,
And that's why they call me Solo Girl!

Cass started to smile. "Not bad," she said. "But what kind of name is Solo Girl?"

"A special name," Bud answered.

Jackson said, "Bud and I figured that a solo is somebody who stands alone, tall and proud—one of a kind."

"Like you, Cass," Bud said.

Cass thought for a moment. "One of a kind. *Solo Girl*, I like that." She smiled. "Run the rhyme by me again," she said.

Jackson and Bud started in. "I got one rope, and that's all I need. . . ."

Cass rocked her shoulders. She sang along with the boys, "I'm trying my best to pick up speed. . . ."

The three of them finished the song together:

I jump alone, while my brothers twirl,
And that's why they call me Solo Girl!

Cass sang the rhyme again. She liked it so much, she sang it over and over. She sang it loud and strong. Jackson and Bud slapped hands. They laughed at how good their made-up rhyme sounded.

Jackson said, "Now let's see what you can do with that rope."

Cass rose from the curb. The rope hung from her hands. "I don't know if I can," she said, shaking her head.

"Here, give it to me," Jackson said. Cass

handed over the rope. Jackson tossed one end to Bud. The boys started to twirl. Cass watched the rope spin. She licked her lips. She wiped her hands on her shorts.

"Jump in!" Bud called.

"I'm getting ready," Cass said, letting out a deep breath.

"Take it slow, sis," Jackson said. "You can do it, for sure."

But Cass held back. She couldn't get herself to make the jump. "My feet will tangle. My legs will get all jumbled. The rope will smack my ankles," she said.

Jackson and Bud kept spinning. Jackson started up with Cass's special rhyme. "I got one rope, and that's all I need. . . ."

Bud joined in, "I'm trying my best to pick up speed. . . ."

The boys kept singing. Like before, Cass started singing too.

I jump alone, while my brothers twirl,
And that's why they call me Solo Girl!

Cass and her brothers sang the song again and again. Jackson and Bud never let the rope rest. Cass tried to jump in. But the rope didn't even make it once around. It tangled up on her knees.

"See what I mean? I'm a jump rope dud," Cass said.

"You just gotta put your mind to it," Jackson said.

"Keep your eyes on the rope," said Bud.

But every time Cass tried, her feet hit the rope.

Then Jackson got an idea. "Use your whistle, Cass."

"My whistle?"

"*Blow* the beat," Jackson said.

Cass shrugged. "Same way I blow to memorize the times tables?"

Bud nodded.

The boys started spinning the rope again.

"We'll do the Solo Girl song, while you work your whistle," Jackson said.

Bud and Jackson started in together. "I got one rope, and that's all I need. . . ."

Cass kept her eyes on the rope. She lifted her whistle to her lips and blew to the

rhythm of her Solo Girl song—*toot, toot, toot, toot* . . .

The rope smacked the sidewalk as it twirled.

Cass's brothers kept on. "I'm trying my best to pick up speed. . . ."

Cass blew out the beat—*toot, toot, toot, toot*—her own special music. One-of-a-kind music. Music that set her feet on the right rhythm. Then she jumped into the rope, slow, but steady.

"You got it, Cass!" Jackson shouted.

"Work it easy, Solo Girl! Don't rush it, now," Bud laughed. The boys sang on for Cass:

I got one rope, and that's all I need.
I'm trying my best to pick up speed.
I jump alone, while my brothers twirl,
And that's why they call me Solo Girl!

Jackson and Bud kept the rope going, no matter what. They kept Cass's jump rope rhyme whirling from their lips, while Cass blew her whistle to keep the beat.

5

Slow-Mo

The next morning, Cass woke before Jackson and Bud. She grabbed her whistle and her jump rope and headed for the door. When she came through the kitchen, Ma Lettie was enjoying a cup of tea. "You look like you're ready for a rabbit race," Ma Lettie said. "Where are you off to in such a hurry, child?"

"To work on my rope jumping, Ma Lettie. Jackson and Bud helped me get the rhythm for one rope, and now I'm trying for two ropes—for double Dutch."

"Not without breakfast, you're not," Ma

Lettie said, rising to make Cass a slice of cinnamon toast.

Cass blew tiny whistle toots as she waited for her toast. Ma Lettie wrapped up the warm bread for Cass and told her to stay close to home. "I'll send your brothers as soon as they wake," Ma Lettie called after Cass.

The street was quiet with the hush of early morning. Cass found a patch of sidewalk on the corner of Haskins Row and Grant Avenue, where she lived.

She ate her toast, then blew her whistle softly, singing her Solo Girl rhyme in her thoughts. Her whistle sent its music into the still morning.

Then a voice broke Cass's song.

"Hey—you with the whistle, I'm trying to work!" The shout came from the front stoop on the corner.

It was Pearl, the girl from Haskins Row, the leader of the Fast Feet Four. She sat cross-legged, a book resting in her lap.

Cass put a quick stop to her whistle. "What are you working on?" she asked.

"Homework—summer school," Pearl called from the stoop. "I gotta do it right, or else."

Cass rested her jump rope on her shoulder. She slid onto the stoop, next to Pearl. "Or else what?" she asked.

"Or else I'm gonna be a slow-mo." Pearl was talking fast, like she was in a big hurry. She shook her head. "A slow-mo ain't no way to be," she said. "I gotta figure this stuff out."

Cass looked down at Pearl's open book. The page was full of numbers. Full of times tables. "My name's Cass," she said. "Me and my brothers and Ma Lettie just moved in over on Grant Avenue."

Pearl folded her arms. "I've seen you checking me out, Cass," she said.

Cass nodded. "I've been watching how you double Dutch, mostly. And looking at your pretty shoelaces."

Pearl pulled a jumbled ball of laces from her hip pocket. "I've got a set in every color," she bragged. "Except purple. I've got only one of those. I lost the other one at the Laundromat. The purple one brings me luck, so I keep it." Pearl rested her hand on her hip. "I may be a slow-mo, but at least I've got a lucky lace."

Cass shrugged. "I never heard of a slow-mo," she said.

"A slow-mo is anybody who can't catch

onto something right away. I'm a slow-mo with math. That's why I'm in summer school," Pearl said.

Cass said, "When it comes to jumping rope, I'm stuck with slow-mo feet. My brothers are trying to help. But the thing is, I can only jump with one rope. I wish I had double-Dutch feet, like you, Pearl."

Pearl shoved her bundle of shoelaces back in her pocket. "Yeah, I'm pretty good at double Dutch."

Cass showed Pearl her whistle. "Sorry I messed up your homework," she said. "But my whistle's what helps me keep the rhythm when I jump. I won it at my school, back home. Won it in a math bee, doing times tables. Ma Lettie even had special words put on it."

Pearl leaned in toward Cass to get a closer look at Cass's whistle. "Can I touch it?" she asked.

Cass nodded.

"'Blessed with the numbers gift'," Pearl read the inscription. "I wish *I* had the numbers gift like *you*."

"Want me to teach you the times tables?" Cass asked.

Pearl bumped her shoulder to Cass. "See, my purple shoelace *is* bringing me luck. How 'bout this—you teach me math, and I'll teach you to double Dutch."

"Deal," Cass said, lifting the book from Pearl's lap.

6

The Secret of the Fives

As the sun rose high over Haskins Row, Cass showed Pearl how to do her times tables.

"Do you know the fives?" Cass asked.

Pearl shook her head. "Nope. It's like I told you, math and I don't mix."

Cass cradled Pearl's math book in her own lap. "When you do the fives, there's a secret," Cass began. "Every answer ends with a zero or a five. And the numbers ending with five or zero switch off—like this." Cass showed Pearl the five-times table in the math book.

"Five times one is—"

"Even *I* know that," Pearl said. "It's five."

"What's five times two, then?" Cass asked.

Pearl started chewing on her pinkie nail. She answered with a question. "Ten?"

Cass nodded. "And what number ends a ten?" she asked.

"Zero," Pearl answered, sure of herself this time.

Cass kept on. "Five times three?" she asked.

Pearl bit her bottom lip. "You're making it hard now, Cass."

Cass tilted the math book so Pearl could see even better. "The answer's gonna end in a zero or a five," she hinted. "And the last answer—two times five—ended with a zero."

"So three times five is gonna end with a five, right?" Pearl said.

"You're catching on, Miss Slow-Mo,"

Cass said.

Pearl was quiet for a moment, working toward the answer.

"Twenty-five?" she said, unsure.

Cass shook her head. "C'mon, now," she said, "think on it."

Then a smile came to Pearl's lips. "I can feel my slow-mo starting to say a fast good-bye—fifteen," she answered.

Cass nudged Pearl. "*Right*," she said. "The secret of the fives is taking hold. And to make it stick, you gotta practice. Do it over and over, till it's dancing in your head."

Pearl leaned into Cass. "Same thing with rope jumping," she said. "Over and over, till your feet are dancing with the sidewalk."

Pearl went inside and came back with her jump rope. She tied its end, along with Cass's rope, to the lamppost at the end of the block. "You turn for me, Cass, and I'll show you how I double Dutch," she said.

Cass watched Pearl's feet weave and bob. "See, I keep my ankles steady and my knee bones greased, loose, like noodles," Pearl instructed.

When Pearl jumped, double Dutch looked as simple as reeling off the fives. "Now, I'll turn, and you jump," Pearl said.

As she watched the two ropes twirl, Cass shook her head. "It's easy for you, Pearl," she said. "But my legs can't do two ropes."

"They can't do two ropes if you're *standing* there," said Pearl.

Cass blew on her whistle, soft and slow at first, then louder. She let her Solo Girl song rise up inside her.

But when Cass jumped in, the ropes caught her ankle. On the second time around, they pulled at her heel. When she tried again, they gave her knees a slap.

Pearl stopped spinning. "You all right, Cass?" she asked.

Cass rubbed the sting from her legs. "As far as double Dutch goes, my slow-mo feet are here to stay," she sighed.

"C'mon, try again," Pearl said.

Cass shook her head. "It's no use."

Every day, for a week, Cass and Pearl met on

the corner. They met early in the morning, when the sun woke.

Cass's jumping got better, but she still couldn't jump more than four times in a row without messing up. "You're thinking too hard about jumping, Cass. You just gotta *do* it," Pearl said, turning the ropes.

"All right," Cass said. "I'm gonna leave my thinking on the sidewalk."

This time, when Cass jumped in, the

ropes made it around ten times before Cass tripped. Even when she stumbled, it was only a little bit.

"You're almost there," Pearl said.

"Thanks to you," said Cass. And with each jump, the all-alone feeling that had been resting in Cass's chest started to slip away.

7

Belly Bone

The next day, the morning's heat came on strong. "It's gonna be hot as blazes today," said Mrs. Carter, who was leaning from her window.

Kids from the neighborhood had started to gather, to cheer on the Fast Feet Four. When Vicky, Robin, and Tammy came to the street, they met Cass. "Cass has a numbers gift. She's been helping me with my math," Pearl said.

Cass was too shy to speak to the other girls at first.

But she showed them her whistle and blew the rhythm of her Solo Girl song.

"When I whistle, I can jump with one rope. But I'm a slow-mo when it comes to double Dutch," Cass said.

Jackson and Bud came down the street, munching on slices of cinnamon toast. "Ma Lettie said we'd find you outside," Bud said, licking butter from his fingers.

Jackson said, "When we heard the whistle, we knew you weren't far away."

Today Pearl and her friends were intro-

ducing a new jump called Belly Bone. Pearl showed Cass and other girls how. She jumped and rubbed her belly at the same time, while turning in a circle. Vicky, Robin, and Tammy learned Belly Bone right away. But Cass didn't even try. "I'll just watch," she said, looking down at the curb.

Now the street corner was full with kids, clapping, stomping, ready for the Fast Feet Four to do their thing. This time Cass stood up front, close to the fun.

Each girl took a turn jumping into the ropes. As each jumped out, the next one jumped in.

Pearl was first. Her feet skipped smoothly and easily. Then Vicky moved to the ropes. She added a finger snap to her jump. Robin did her jumps touching her toes each time. Tammy jumped in after her. She jumped and sang the Fast Feet Four song.

As usual, the folks who had gathered

on the street spoke out.

"There they go again—jammin'!"

"The Fast Feet Four keep getting better and better!"

"Those girls are faster than a taxi!"

Cass, Jackson, and Bud looked on. Cass's feet tapped out a beat on the sidewalk. Bud poked Jackson. Then Jackson elbowed Cass. "Try it out, sis," Jackson said.

Among the shouts and cheers, Cass stepped forward. She tapped Pearl on the shoulder. "I'm gonna give it another try," she said.

Cass was still tapping her toes. Pearl looked down at Cass's feet and smiled. "Girl, it seems like your feet are itching to jump," she said. "When Tammy is done, jump right on in. And give us some of that whistle music you make."

Jackson and Bud watched and waited. Their eyes never left Cass. When Cass glanced over at them, she looked scared. Bud and Jackson waved Cass on. "You can do it,

Cass," they said.

Pearl gave Cass a gentle push. "Your turn," she said.

At first, the ropes spun alone, empty with no jumper. Cass heard somebody whisper, "I think that girl's gonna give it a try."

Before Cass jumped in, Pearl pulled the purple shoelace from her bunch. "Use this to wear your whistle," Pearl said.

Cass untied her whistle string, then pushed the purple shoelace through the whistle's loop. She looked over at her brothers one more time, slid her whistle between her lips, and blinked back her doubt.

8

Sweet Music

Quick as a match spark, Cass jumped in. She jumped slowly at first. But she blew her whistle to find the double-time beat of the two ropes.

The ropes were a blur of white circling over Cass's head. She jumped and jumped and jumped. Her feet didn't snag, and her ankles were strong enough to keep up.

"Who's that girl?" somebody asked.

"Her name is Cass," Pearl said. "She's new around here."

Jackson said to Pearl, "Looks like Cass is catching on pretty good."

"You mean it looks like Solo Girl is catching on," Bud said.

Cass could feel the fun of double Dutch swelling up inside her. While she jumped, the people watching took notice. Angela, who was spinning the ropes said, "Wow, that new girl sure can go!"

"Got it goin' *on*," said Dina, who spun

from the other side.

Mrs. Carter said, "Another fast-footed child to grace our street."

Mr. Lamont, the ice cream man, called out from his cart, "I've seen that child practicing her jumping every morning this week. She deserves a cone on me."

Even Ma Lettie had come to the corner to watch. "That's my Cass," she said, "blessed from her head to her knees to her ankles to her feet."

Cass could hear everybody sending her kind words. That made her jump even better—and faster. While Cass jumped, Pearl called her friends together. They gathered on the corner. When Cass finally jumped out, Pearl waved her over. Cass was breathing heavily, but her feet still tapped on the street. She didn't want to stop jumping.

Vicky said, "We can always use new jumpers."

"And with your whistle, your jumping's

really special," Robin said.

"You're a double Dutcher with style," said Tammy.

Pearl asked, "Want to join the Fast Feet Four?"

"Do I ever!" Cass said. Pearl swung her arm around Cass's shoulder. "That makes us the Fast Feet *Five*," she said.

Jackson and Bud walked over to give Cass her free ice cream cone. "These are my brothers," Cass said. "They're the first ones who taught me how to jump."

"You must be good teachers," Pearl said.

"Yeah, we are," Jackson said, smiling at Bud.

"Not only that," Bud said, pulling a notepad from his back pocket, "we're good at making up jump-rope rhymes too."

"The Fast Feet Five and the Talented Two," Pearl said.

Everybody laughed.

From that day on, Haskins Row had a new double-Dutch team and a new jump-rope chant to go with it. Jackson and Bud worked for hours writing the perfect rhyme. Cass added her whistle to give the beat a pop.

Morning to night, you could hear the new Fast Feet Five rhyme coming from

Haskins Row. It rose high over the rooftop gardens and smokestack chimneys. It was sweet music that made the whole neighborhood sing.

The song went like this:

We call ourselves the Fast Feet Five.
When we jump, our ropes come alive.
There's Vicky and Robin and Tammy and Pearl
And Cass, who we call Solo Girl!

Andrea Davis Pinkney

When I was growing up, I lived on a street in Gaithersburg, Maryland. Whenever I think back to that special place, I hear music. Not the kind of music that played on the radio, but street music: the quiet scratch of a metal snow shovel; the hiss of bike tires on the sidewalk; the giggly chatter of me and my girl-friends; and the distant holler of my mom calling me in for supper.

Solo Girl is a slice of these sweet musical memories.

Hop to It!

Jump right into these puzzle pages and let the fun begin!

Rhyme Time

Jumping rope is fun when you've got a beat. Cass found that out when she learned to jump rope in time to rhymes. Finish these. Then, look for the picture of each word in the scene below.

1. Up in the night sky
Not near, but far
It shines and twinkles
We call it a _____.

2. It bounces high and bounces low
It knows not where it wants to go
Be it summer, winter, spring, or fall
It's so much fun playing with a _____.

3. Flying gracefully through the air
Seeming not to have a care
Shhhh, it landed, don't say a word
Don't scare off this beautiful _____.

4. With whiskers so straight and a bushy tail
He drinks warm milk right out of a pail
Then curls up and rests in the sun on a mat
What a cute and cuddly, friendly old _____.

All Tied Up!

It's not much fun jumping rope when your rope's all tangled up. Help these kids untangle their ropes. Follow each jump rope to see which rope belongs to whom.

If you liked *Solo Girl*, look for these books in your library or bookstore:

The Best, Worst Day by Bonnie Graves
Lucy wants Maya, the new girl in her class with curly brown hair and pierced ears, to be her best friend, but how can Lucy get her attention?

I Hate My Best Friend by Ruth Rosner
Annie and Nini are super best friends, and they do everything together until the day Nini decides unexpectedly that she doesn't have time for old friends anymore.

Jenius: The Amazing Guinea Pig by Dick King-Smith
Judy is sure that Jenius, her prodigious guinea pig, will stun her class at show-and-tell . . . as long as Jenius is smart enough to stay away from scary cats.

Mystery of the Tooth Gremlin by Bonnie Graves
Jesse is excited about losing his first tooth, but when he leaves it on his desk, it mysteriously disappears.

No Room for Francie by Maryann Macdonald
With six siblings, Francie never has her own space, so how will she produce the private clubhouse she's planned?

Spoiled Rotten by Barthe DeClements
The second-grade teacher will not tolerate Andy's spoiled-rotten attitude; will his best friend, Scott, stand up for him in front of their classmates?